Andre Agassi

Additional Titles in the Sports Reports *Series*

Andre Agassi
Star Tennis Player
(0-89490-798-0)

Troy Aikman
Star Quarterback
(0-89490-927-4)

Roberto Alomar
Star Second Baseman
(0-7660-1079-1)

Charles Barkley
Star Forward
(0-89490-655-0)

Terrell Davis
Star Running Back
(07660-1331-6)

Dale Earnhardt
Star Race Car Driver
(0-7660-1335-9)

Brett Favre
Star Quarter Back
(0-7660-1332-4)

Jeff Gordon
Star Race Car Driver
(0-7660-1083-X)

Wayne Gretzky
Star Center
(0-89490-930-4)

Ken Griffey, Jr.
Star Outfielder
(0-89490-802-2)

Scott Hamilton
Star Figure Skater
(0-7660-1236-0)

Anfernee Hardaway
Star Guard
(0-7660-1234-4)

Grant Hill
Star Forward
(0-7660-1078-3)

Michael Jordan
Star Guard
(0-89490-482-5)

Shawn Kemp
Star Forward
(0-89490-929-0)

Jason Kidd
Star Guard
(0-7660-1333-2)

Mario Lemieux
Star Center
(0-89490-932-0)

Karl Malone
Star Forward
(0-89490-931-2)

Dan Marino
Star Quarterback
(0-89490-933-9)

Mark McGwire
Star Home Run Hitter
(0-7660-1329-4)

Mark Messier
Star Center
(0-89490-801-4)

Reggie Miller
Star Guard
(0-7660-1082-1)

Chris Mullin
Star Forward
(0-89490-486-8)

Hakeem Olajuwon
Star Center
(0-89490-803-0)

Shaquille O'Neal
Star Center
(0-89490-656-9)

Gary Payton
Star Guard
(0-7660-1330-8)

Scottie Pippen
Star Forward
(0-7660-1080-5)

Jerry Rice
Star Wide Receiver
(0-89490-928-2)

Cal Ripken, Jr.
Star Shortstop
(0-89490-485-X)

David Robinson
Star Center
(0-89490-483-3)

Barry Sanders
Star Running Back
(0-89490-484-1)

Deion Sanders
Star Athlete
(0-89490-652-6)

Junior Seau
Star Linebacker
(0-89490-800-6)

Emmitt Smith
Star Running Back
(0-89490-653-4)

Frank Thomas
Star First Baseman
(0-89490-659-3)

Thurman Thomas
Star Running Back
(0-89490-445-0)

Chris Webber
Star Forward
(0-89490-799-9)

Tiger Woods
Star Golfer
(0-7660-1081-3)

Steve Young
Star Quarterback
(0-89490-654-2)

SPORTS REPORTS

Andre Agassi

Star Tennis Player

Ron Knapp

Enslow Publishers, Inc.
40 Industrial Road
Box 398
Berkeley Heights, NJ 07922
USA

PO Box 38
Aldershot
Hants GU12 6BP
UK

http://www.enslow.com

Library of Congress Cataloging-in-Publication Data

Knapp, Ron.
Andre Agassi : star tennis player / Ron Knapp.
p. cm. —(Sports reports)
Includes bibliographical references and index.
Summary: Profiles the personal life and tennis career of the showy winner of the 1992 Wimbledon championship.
ISBN 0-89490-798-0
1. Agassi, Andre, 1970– —Juvenile literature. 2. Tennis players—Biography—Juvenile literature. [1. Agassi, Andre, 1970– . 2. Tennis players.]
I. Title. II. Series.
GV994.A43K53 1997
796.342'092—dc20
[B] 96-9134
CIP
AC

Printed in the United States of America

10 9 8 7 6 5 4 3

To Our Readers:
All Internet addresses in this book were active and appropriate when we went to press. Any comments or suggestions can be sent by e-mail to Comments@enslow.com or to the address on the back cover.

Illustration Credits: Michael Baz, pp. 9, 13, 15, 22, 24, 30, 33, 34, 38, 40, 46, 48, 50, 59, 65, 67, 72, 73, 76, 77, 80, 83, 87, 89, 92.

Cover Photo: Michael Baz

Contents

Chapter 1

Wimbledon Is Wonderful

In 1992, twenty-two-year-old Andre Agassi was one of the most famous and popular athletes in the world. Many tennis fans thought he was the most exciting—and coolest—player in the game.

At tournaments, he was constantly surrounded by crowds of teenage girls who treated him like he was a rock star. Thousands of teenage boys imitated the flashy way he dressed and wore their hair long like his.

By 1992, despite his popularity and the controversy surrounding almost everything he did, Agassi had still not won any of the Grand Slam tournaments—Wimbledon and the Opens in France, Australia, and the United States. He had made it to three Grand Slam finals, but lost each time. Besides being known as a flamboyant, exciting star, he was beginning to have a reputation as a choker. He couldn't win the important matches.

Andre's reputation was about to change. In June, he joined the world's best players at Wimbledon's All-England Championships, the most important Grand Slam tournament of them all. Since 1877, players had been competing for the annual title on Wimbledon's grass courts just outside London.

At first, it looked like the same old story. Andre was repeatedly mobbed by his young fans, and the reporters paid more attention to his outfits and his hairstyle than to his tennis. When he showed up to play in a white cap, the photographers went wild. Why was he covering his head? Was he attempting to start a new style? Was he trying to hide the fact that he was losing his hair? It was no big deal, Andre explained. The sun was bright, and he didn't want to wear sunglasses, so he put on a cap.

The Grand Slam events are all single-elimination tournaments. As soon as a player loses, he's out. The winners keep playing until there's only one player left, the champion. Agassi played well enough in the early rounds of the tournament to make it to the quarterfinals against Boris Becker, the German star who had won the title in 1985, 1986, and 1989. Most

FACT

The All-England Croquet and Lawn Tennis Club held its first tournament at Wimbledon in 1877. More than one hundred years later, it still captures the attention of the world when competition begins each summer late in June. It is the only Grand Slam event played on grass. It's also the only tournament with a strict dress code. All players—even Andre Agassi—must wear white outfits on the courts.

Agassi was paired against John McEnroe in the 1992 Wimbledon semi-finals. McEnroe had already won the Wimbledon Tournament three times.

tennis experts were sure Agassi didn't have a chance against the former champion.

As expected, Becker won the first set, 6–4, but then Andre took control of the match. Staying far from the net, back by the baseline, he hammered his powerful shots all over the court and won the next two sets, 6–2, 6–2.

Men players need three sets to win a Grand Slam match, so Agassi was only one set away from the biggest victory of his career. Becker, however, hung tough and was leading 4–3 when rain began to fall and the match was postponed. The next day, when play resumed, the German quickly completed a 6–4 set, and the match was tied. Many of the reporters prepared to write stories about Agassi choking and losing another big match.

Then Andre surprised almost everybody by running Becker ragged in the final set, beating him 6–3. As his fans screamed their approval, he bowed shyly, then buried his face in a towel. For a while, he didn't seem to believe he had won. "This isn't just a Grand Slam," he kept repeating. "It's Wimbledon."[1]

In the semifinals, he would have to face John McEnroe, another three-time champion (1981, 1983, 1984). Many fans figured that Agassi would have more than he could handle against the veteran star. McEnroe had been a Wimbledon champ when

Andre was only eleven years old. Besides, Agassi didn't even like playing on grass. Probably he had just been lucky to beat Becker.

Once again, the young man with the white cap over his long hair surprised almost everybody. His quick shots rocketed down one side of the court, then the other. McEnroe ran back and forth, trying to reach them, but over and over, he had to watch them sail by. More than a few times, he found himself sprawled on the grass, staring in disbelief at the great shots he couldn't reach. Agassi made the great champion look like a tired old man as he won 6–4, 6–2, 6–2.

Reporters asked if he was sorry he had ruined what was probably McEnroe's last shot at a Wimbledon title. "I think I would insult him to say I felt bad," he said. "I happened to get the right shots at the right time. Things went my way. It's tough to feel bad about it."[2]

In the final, Andre would face Goran Ivanisevic, whose blazing serve had helped him beat Pete Sampras in the semifinals 6–7, 7–6, 6–4, 6–2. Ivanisevic's serve was the toughest in men's tennis. In the semifinals, he had 36 aces, serves so hard that Sampras couldn't even touch them. When he was serving, he had never lost a game. In fact, Sampras never got more than two points in a game against his serve.

Agassi had a reputation for playing a tough

game from the baseline and being able to return almost any ball hit at him, but could he really handle Ivanisevic's brutal serve on Wimbledon's grass in the biggest match of his life?

Andre hung tough in the long, exciting opening set. After twelve games, it was tied 6–6, and they had to play a tiebreaker. That meant that they would keep playing until one player had at least seven points and two more than his opponent. Ivanisevic finally was able to win the tiebreaker, 10–8, to take the first set.

As Andre rested briefly on the sidelines, he must have been thinking about the 11 aces his opponent had zinged by him. He had played some of the best tennis of his career, and he had still lost the set. The fans at Wimbledon's center court wondered how upset he would be. Was it time for Agassi to choke and lose the whole match?

No. Not this time.

Andre walked back onto the court and took over. He won the next two sets 6–4, 6–4. Now Ivanisevic was the one in trouble. Agassi was a set away from tennis's greatest prize.

Then Ivanisevic got hot. He took just seventeen minutes to destroy Andre 6–1, in the fourth set. His 10 aces made him look almost unstoppable. The match would be decided in the fifth set.

In the 1992 Wimbledon Final, Agassi faced Goran Ivanisevic, who has one of the fastest serves in tennis.

Both men were tired, but they were playing fine tennis, and the fans at center court were loving the action. It was the most exciting Wimbledon men's final in years. When the final set was tied 3–3, it looked like it was going to go down to the wire.

In the back of his mind, Andre couldn't forget that he had never won a Grand Slam tournament. "I've had my chances to fulfill a lot of my dreams, but I haven't come through before," he said later.[3] Then, in the next game, he fell behind a break point. Ivanisevic needed only one more point to win the game.

Andre knew he had to hang tough. On the next point, he raced to the net and slammed an unhittable winner. Then he delivered an ace of his own. Soon the game was his.

After each player won his own serve, Agassi led 5–4. Finally he was confident. "If I could get him down to one final game, I liked my chances."[4] Finally, that was all he needed.

Andre waited on center court for another of Ivanisevic's blistering serves, but the first one missed and so did the second! Double fault! Point to Agassi!

Andre switched sides and watched the next two serves miss, too. Double fault again! He was up 30–love.

Ivanisevic got his serve under control and tied

Lining up his shot, Agassi looks to hit a backhand winner. During the 1992 Wimbledon final, his backhand proved to be the winning shot.

the game by winning the next two points. Agassi was able to return the next serve, and Ivanisevic popped a soft shot back. Andre attacked the ball, slashing it out of reach for the point! He led 40–30. It was match point. If he could win the next point, the match and the title were his.

Agassi backhanded the serve right back to Ivanisevic, who slashed a backhand of his own. "I was sure it was going in," he said, "but it went into the net. Then he was on the ground and I was still standing."[5]

As the crowd jumped to its feet, Andre dropped his racket and fell on his knees. "I can't believe it," he said.[6]

Then he fell on his face and lay on center court. When he stood up, there were tears in his eyes. The cheers grew louder. Ivanisevic jumped over the net and ran to him. "Listen, man, you deserve it," he said. "You played great."[7]

Ivanisevic was right. Andre Agassi had finally done it. This time he had won the big match. Now he was the champion of Wimbledon. "It's the greatest title in the world," he said, "the greatest achievement I've ever made."[8]

Nobody could argue with that.

Chapter 2

Agassi's Early Life

Emmanuel "Mike" Agassi has always loved tennis.

He first saw the sport when he was growing up in Iran, a Middle Eastern country more than seven thousand miles from the United States. Luckily for Mike, he lived near a pair of dirt tennis courts. They were behind a church run by American missionaries. When he was a little boy, Mike loved to watch American soldiers playing the game. He spent so much time around the court that he was given the job of watering it and keeping it in good condition.

Over the years, he learned to play tennis himself. He was a fine athlete, good enough, in fact, to be a member of his country's Olympic boxing teams in 1948 and 1952.

Mike Agassi gave up boxing in the 1950s and moved to the United States. First he settled in Chicago, Illinois, where he worked as a waiter in a hotel restaurant. By then, he and his wife, Betty, had two children, Rita and Phillip. The family didn't stay in Chicago for long, because Mike didn't like the cold weather.

Even though he was thousands of miles from the dirt courts he had loved in Iran, Mike had never given up his passion for tennis. Now that he was in a new country with a young family, he had a dream. He would find a home where the weather was always warm and he could teach his children to play tennis year-round.

Soon the Agassi family moved to Las Vegas, Nevada, a city rapidly filling with hotels and gambling casinos. Betty was hired by the state of Nevada to work with immigrants moving into the area, and Mike got a job in one of the casinos. He worked each night until 3:00 A.M., then hurried home for a few hours of sleep. At 7:00 A.M., he drove his two children to a hotel tennis court where they practiced until it was time for school. As soon as school was out, the three of them returned to the court for a few more hours. Mike hoped that all this work would turn his kids into tennis champions.

Then on April 29, 1970, Rita and Phillip got a

FACT

Until Nevada legalized gambling in 1931, Las Vegas was a small town. Today it's filled with casinos, where people can play cards or slot machines. Entertainers and sporting events like boxing also draw thousands of visitors to the city. Today Las Vegas is one of the most popular tourist destinations in the U. S.

baby brother named Andre. Their father went right to work. He didn't want to wait until Andre was big enough to go to the tennis courts. In fact, he didn't even wait until the baby was out of his crib. "As soon as Andre could open his eyes, I got a tennis racket, attached it to the ceiling, and tied a ball to it with a string, so that it hung down above his crib," Mike said. "Then, whenever I walked by, I would just give the ball a little tap and it would swing back and forth over him."[1] He was sure this was a great way to teach his son to follow the ball with his eyes.

"When he could sit up in a high chair, I took a ping-pong paddle and split it down the middle so it was very light and taped it to his hand. Then I'd take a balloon and put a little bit of water in it and toss the balloon at him until he learned to meet it with his paddle."[2]

When Andre could move around in a walker, his father gave him a full-sized racket. The little boy spent his days rolling through the house, swinging his racket at whatever he could reach. Once he whacked a salt shaker into a glass door.

Soon after he learned to walk, Andre and his racket were on the tennis court. When he was three, he could hit the ball back and forth over the net with his father. When professional players came to Las Vegas for tournaments, Mike made sure Andre was practicing on a nearby court. Sometimes there were more people watching the cute little boy with the big racket and long brown hair than were watching the pros. Everybody was very impressed except Pancho Gonzales, a veteran player who would one day marry Rita Agassi. "When I first saw Andre at two or three years old," he said, "I didn't think he was going to be any good."[3] People laughed at Gonzales's remark. How many three-year-olds can even swing a full-size racket?

FACT

A forehand shot occurs when a player swings at a ball on the same side of his body as the hand with the racket. When the ball is on the opposite side of his body, he must hit it with a backhand shot.

Before he was four years old, Andre was hitting balls with Bobby Riggs, the 1939 Wimbledon champion, on the court of the Tropicana Hotel. As usual, he was surrounded by a small crowd. "I remember being watched," he said. "And I remember liking it."[4]

On his fourth birthday in 1974, Andre celebrated by hitting balls with Jimmy Connors, who would win the Australian Open, Wimbledon, and the U.S. Open that year. Two years later, after working out with Ilie Nastase, the 1972 U.S. Open champ, Andre signed his first autograph.

Mike Agassi wanted Andre to be much more than just a little kid playing tennis with the superstars. He wanted his boy to be a tennis superstar himself. Rita and Phillip were good, but Mike had the feeling that Andre was going to be great.

Mr. Agassi was devoting most of his time and

money to making his children stars. He saved $860 to buy a machine that would shoot balls back at the kids. Soon he saved enough to buy two more. Then Rita, Phillip, and Andre could spend hours every day trying to hit back shot after shot zinging at them at more than 100 miles per hour. The two older children hit seven to eight thousand balls a week. Andre was beginning to spend even more time on the court; his total was around fourteen thousand.

"My dad kept telling me to hit harder and harder, and that's exactly what I did," he said.[5] Mike figured that the best way for Andre to get a strong shot was for him to attack every ball with all his might. "Hit the ball as hard as you can," he said. "Worry about keeping it in later."[6]

All the practice began to pay off. When he was seven years old, Andre entered—and won—his first tournament by beating players who were as much as two years older than him. He also won his next eight tournaments. Soon his mother was driving him five hundred miles to matches in California.

Andre loved tennis, and he didn't usually mind practicing, but his father was always a tough, demanding coach. He screamed at his children, always demanding that they work harder and get better. When they lost, he was furious. When they won, he didn't praise them. After all, that's what he expected them to do.

The pressure seemed to bother Rita the most. When she lost an important match at a tournament, she vomited blood. When she was thirteen years old, she already had bleeding ulcers, but she kept playing and trying to please her father. She kept at it until she was nineteen and won her first small pro tournament. Almost as soon as she had the trophy in her hands, she decided to give up the sport. She married Pancho Gonzales and quit speaking with her father.

Andre was just eleven when his sister gave up

In order to become a tennis star, Andre Agassi had to put in many hours of practice. As a young boy he would sometimes hit 14,000 balls a week.

tournament tennis. Even then, his father never changed his approach to tennis. He kept his sons practicing for hours every day. By then, their little sister, Tami, was old enough to take up the game, too. Soon Phillip would enroll at the University of Nevada-Las Vegas, where he would play on the tennis team.

Most of Mike's attention was focused on his youngest son. Even though Rita had quit, even if Phillip might not be good enough to be a pro, their father was positive that Andre was going to be a star. Many other people agreed. After the boy volleyed with Bjorn Borg, the winner of five straight Wimbledon titles (1976–1980), Borg's coach said that Andre was a better younger player than Borg had been.

The endless hours of practice continued. When Andre wasn't eating, sleeping, or in school, he was on the tennis court. Soon his parents were driving him all over the country, looking for tougher and tougher competition. In the stands at the tournaments, Mike was just as loud and as intense as he was on the practice court. Once he even got into a fistfight with the father of another young player.

When thirteen-year-old Andre lost a quarterfinal match in a national tournament, Mike was so disappointed and disgusted that he dragged his son off the court even before he could get his trophy. After Andre took a disappointing 3rd place at a

A lot of pressure was put on Agassi to become a great tennis player. He often had to sacrifice things that most kids like to do in order to concentrate on tennis.

tournament in San Diego, his father angrily threw his trophy into a garbage can. "Mr. Agassi never thought Andre was playing well enough," said David Kass, one of the boy's friends. "He always thought Andre could play better."[7]

The pressure was always there. Andre could never relax and enjoy his success. His whole life revolved around tennis. There was hardly ever time to just goof around with his friends and enjoy being a kid. Years later, Mike admitted that he had made mistakes in the way he had raised and trained his youngest son. "The real sacrifice," he said, "was Andre's childhood."[8]

When Andre was a youngster, Mike's energy was focused on making him a professional star. He began wondering if he should find an experienced coach for the boy. Then he came across Nick Bollettieri, a coach who ran an academy, or boarding school, for some of the best junior players in the world.

"My father saw this story on Nick on *60 Minutes* where it showed him making these little kids cry and everything," Agassi said later, "and thought that was the place for me."[9] When he was thirteen years old, Andre left his family in Las Vegas to move across the country to Bollettieri's academy in Bradenton, Florida.

Chapter 3

At the Tennis Academy

Nick Bollettieri was a man with a dream. He wanted to coach the best tennis players in the world, but more than that, he wanted to be the one who made them great. To do that, he had to find them when they were still young.

Bollettieri could have concentrated on one or two fine young players, but that would have been too risky. What if, after years of coaching, a player suffered a career-ending injury? Or what if, despite all Bollettieri's efforts, the youngster never developed into a top player?

The coach decided not to put all of his eggs into just a couple of baskets. Instead of concentrating on just one or two players, he would work with dozens.

That would greatly increase his chances of developing a superstar or two.

Sometimes young players find it difficult to devote themselves to endless hours of practice. They would rather go to dances, belong to clubs, or just hang out with their friends. Sometimes parents prevent the athletes from improving by arguing with coaches or by putting too much pressure on their children.

Bollettieri wanted to have his young players all to himself. He didn't want them to be bothered by parents or friends or school activities. He wanted them to be able to focus all their energy on tennis, and he wanted to be the one giving the lessons and putting on the pressure.

That's why he started the Nick Bollettieri Tennis Academy in Bradenton, Florida. It was a huge complex with classrooms, a cafeteria, and dormitories for 175 youngsters, but most important of all, there were 46 tennis courts. Students attended regular school classes in the morning, but by 1:00 P.M. they were all on the courts. That's where they spent most of the rest of the day.

Bollettieri was almost broke when he opened the academy in 1978, but he was soon able to convince many rich parents to pay the $20,000 annual tuition to enroll their children. He also convinced the companies that make Prince rackets and Penn tennis balls to keep the school supplied with free equipment. They also paid him a good deal of money for the privilege of being the academy's official sponsors. The companies figured that if Bollettieri's students would use their products, it would help make the rackets and balls popular among fans.

Bollettieri used the money to improve the academy's facilities and to give full scholarships to the best players. That's how Andre Agassi was able to enroll. Mr. and Mrs. Agassi weren't wealthy enough to raise the $20,000 tuition themselves. Andre was such a great player that Bollettieri was willing to let him attend for free.

Andre was good, but there were several better players at the school. In fact, what his classmates usually remember today about him isn't his tennis playing but his behavior. "I was just so obnoxious," he admits.[1] Far away from his parents, thirteen-year-old Andre had nobody around to make him behave. Bollettieri and his staff were focused on the boy's tennis ability. They didn't want to waste time worrying about his behavior.

Andre pulled some pretty wild stunts. "When I was fourteen," he said, "I dared a kid to shave his head. 'You shave yours and I'll shave mine,' I said. We did, and from then on, I just started wearing my hair differently."[2] His long brown hair was gone, and for a while, Andre looked like Michael Jordan. As the hair grew back in, he decided to give up the bald look. For a while, he experimented with the Mohawk look and patches of brightly dyed hair.

When he got tired of trying to shock people with weird hairstyles, he began trying out other strange fashions. In the 1980s, while he was at the academy, most men and boy players wore simple white shorts and shirts. Not Andre. He played the finals of a tournament in Pensacola, Florida, wearing jeans. He topped the outfit off with eye makeup and an earring.

His tournament attire was too much for Bollettieri and the other coaches. They thought his strange outfits were beginning to interfere with his tennis. Instead of trying to look weird, why couldn't Andre just devote his energy and talent to improving his game?

Their criticism made the boy furious. What right did they have to tell him how to dress? Andre had had enough. He packed his suitcase and started walking to the airport. He had decided to fly home to Las Vegas. On the way to the airport, he finally changed his mind and turned around, but that didn't mean he was going to be a model pupil.

Sometimes Andre just got lonesome. It wasn't easy being thousands of miles away from his home.

Agassi has always been known for looking different than most tennis players. When he was a teenager, he once played in a tournament wearing jeans, an earring, and eye makeup.

Once he sold his tennis equipment so he could buy a plane ticket from Las Vegas to Bradenton for his friend Perry Rogers.

In his three years at Bollettieri's academy, Agassi was never able to concentrate for long on his game. "Andre had just had enough of the juniors [competition]," said his classmate David Wheaton. "He blew it off."[3] Instead of becoming one of the school's top prospects, he was just another player. Instead of focusing on his tennis skills, he seemed to concentrate on new ways to make people dislike him.

Most tennis players keep their mouths shut when they're playing. Not young Andre. He liked to "talk trash" to his opponents. He enjoyed getting them mad at him. "A player had to be willing to take a lot not to get in a fight with me," he said.[4]

Agassi also enjoyed slamming shots off players too slow to get out of the way. "If Andre got a high ball," said Wheaton, "you knew exactly where he was going to put it—at your head."[5]

If he couldn't get his opponent angry, he got mad himself. It wasn't unusual to see him smash his racket down onto the court. In one match alone, he wrecked seven rackets. Sometimes he broke them against walls. A few times he threw them into nearby swimming pools. Years later, he estimated that he intentionally broke about a racket a week while he

FACT

When a player is close to the net, his opponent will often try to hit a *lob*, a long, high, soft shot that goes over his head, forcing him to retreat. The opposite of a lob is an *overhead slam*, in which the player swings down hard to blast the ball over the net.

was at the academy. Luckily for Agassi and Bollettieri, the Prince company kept supplying free rackets.

Andre was not a happy young man. Ever since he was a baby, his father had insisted that he spend almost all of his time practicing and thinking about tennis. At the school, Bollettieri was the same way. Agassi's life seemed to be an endless series of practices and matches. All that work wasn't doing much to improve his game or to make him happy. "It was a living hell," he said years later.[6]

Andre decided that the only way to get out of his unhappy rut was to play more tennis—as a professional. He wanted to play against older players for money in important tournaments around the world. Athletes who do well in professional tournaments earn thousands of dollars. That would have to be more fun than staying at the academy. The problem was that it took a lot of money to become a professional tennis player. Andre would have to buy all his own equipment and pay for traveling expenses as he journeyed from tournament to tournament. His parents weren't rich enough to do that, and, of course, Andre could hardly expect to raise the money himself. He was still only fifteen years old, and he'd never had a real job. All he could do was play tennis.

Bollettieri came to his rescue by introducing the

On May 1, 1986, Agassi left the Nick Bollettieri Tennis Academy at the age of sixteen in order to become a professional tennis player.

When Andre Agassi decided to turn pro, Jimmy Connors was one of the brightest stars in men's tennis. If Agassi wanted to be able to compete for major titles, he would have to beat players like Connors.

teenager to representatives of the Nike shoe company. If Andre would wear their shoes while he competed, they agreed to pay him $25,000 a year. That was enough to buy his equipment and cover his expenses in the early stages of his professional career. After a few months, he figured, he'd be earning so much in tournaments that money would no longer be a problem.

On May 1, 1986, just two days after his sixteenth birthday, Andre Agassi left the academy to become a professional tennis player. The move took some courage and a lot of confidence. Most athletes who try to become professionals aren't good enough to make enough money to stay in the game. Andre wasn't even a fully grown man, he was just a skinny teenager who would be trying to make a living playing against superstars like Jimmy Connors and John McEnroe. Most boys his age were playing high school sports, going to school, and holding down part-time jobs at places like grocery stores and restaurants.

"Here was this kid who had turned pro at 16 who didn't even have a high school diploma," said Mary Jane Wheaton, mother of Andre's classmate David Wheaton. "Who had been geared to do one thing his whole life. Can you imagine? If Andre didn't make it in tennis, he was stuck."[7]

Chapter 4

His Early Career

Andre Agassi's first few weeks as a professional tennis player went very well. Even though he was just a sixteen-year-old rookie, he won enough matches before being eliminated in his first two tournaments to earn $11,500.

His older brother, Phillip, was traveling with him from tournament to tournament. He made sure Andre's equipment was organized and that he always met schedules for matches and airline travel. Phillip was also there to keep an eye on his little brother and to keep him company. Much of the time Andre's coach, Nick Bollettieri, was there, too. Even though Andre had wanted to escape the academy, he still valued Bollettieri's advice. During breaks in his schedule, he even returned to the academy to practice.

Andre's good fortune on the tennis court didn't last for long. He began losing almost all his matches. In the eight months after August 1986, he only won one. The pro tour was tougher than he had imagined. Bigger, stronger players with years of experience had little trouble beating him. Andre also had some trouble getting used to the different court surfaces. He had grown up playing on paved hard courts like the ones in most American parks and schoolyards. On the tour, he sometimes had to play on tricky clay courts, much softer surfaces that slowed down the

STATS

Active Players on ATP Tour with most Hardcourt Titles Through 1996.

Player	Titles
Andre Agassi	25
Pete Sampras	25
Boris Becker	16
Michael Chang	15
Jim Courier	14

balls after they bounced. Of course, Wimbledon, the biggest tournament of them all, was played on grass, a surface much faster than hard courts.

Physically, Agassi wasn't really ready to play professional tennis. Not only was he younger and smaller than almost all the other players; his conditioning wasn't nearly as good. Despite his years of practice, he wasn't even flexible enough to bend over and touch his toes. When he ran after his opponents' shots, he moved unsteadily. Even his head bobbed back and forth. He had trouble making fast starts and stops. When he finished matches, his knees were usually sore.

Andre's worst problem was probably his lack of mental toughness. Sometimes he wasted his enormous talent by getting angry or by trying to make the fans laugh or just by losing interest in his matches. It wasn't unusual for him to quit trying in the middle of a set, then tell reporters, "I just didn't feel it inside."[1]

Andre's attitude made his brother angry. "You've got to develop the mental discipline," Phillip told him.[2] Andre didn't listen. Once he purposely blew a set, losing 0-6 to John McEnroe, who was furious. "Insulting, immature, a cop-out," he said. "I don't think that's showing respect for your opponent."[3]

In July 1987, after a first-round loss at a tournament in Washington, D. C., Andre had had

Watching his opponent's every move, Agassi awaits the serve. When Agassi first turned pro he was not ready mentally or physically for the pro game.

enough. "The game isn't for me," he told Phillip and Bollettieri. "I can't play good tennis."[4] He ran from the court to a nearby park, where he gave his rackets to a pair of old men playing checkers.[5] Then he sat down at a table and began to cry. A friend who was also a minister walked over to the table to comfort him. Don't quit, he told him. Just keep trying.[6] It wasn't the first time the minister had talked to Andre about his talent. Eventually he helped Andre form a new attitude about his sport. "I am blessed with a talent," Agassi said, "and I have an obligation to the Lord to make the most of it."[7]

His new attitude was very evident to the fans and other players. Now he always tried to win and to show good sportsmanship even when he was losing. Sometimes he even clapped when an opponent hit a great shot past him. "Suddenly I realized I could still be competitive and say 'nice shot.' The thought of losing doesn't bother me now. It only bothers me if I haven't given 100 percent effort. So the pressure is off. If I lose, I lose. I now know that if I stay positive and keep on working, my talent will eventually come out."[8]

Agassi had become a born-again Christian. He said his new attitude was based on his religion. "What Christianity has offered in my life is peace of mind and understanding that it's no big deal if you get beat."[9]

FACT

Love is the proper tennis term for zero. *Deuce* means the score is tied. The score advances from love to 15, 30, and 40. After that, unless it's a deuce game, the player with 40 will win if he gets the next point. If it's a deuce game at 40, the winner has to go ahead by two points.

As time wore on, Andre's conditioning improved and he became more comfortable against professional competition. By the end of 1987, at the age of seventeen, Andre moved up to become the 25th ranked player in the world.

To get tougher physically, he began regular workouts with Fritz Nau, one of the academy's conditioning coaches. For hours, he high-stepped through tires, one at a time. He practiced taking five quick steps backward, then stopping. Over and over, he jumped rope, being careful to keep his head still. He also stretched and lifted weights. Andre improved his flexibility and strength and gained a much smoother running style. "Now he's using just the right amount of energy," Nau said, "and there's no wasted motion."[10]

Late in 1987, Agassi's new attitude and his improved physical condition helped make him a winner again. In an exhibition match in Florida, he beat Jimmy Connors, the veteran star he had first played on his fourth birthday. He earned $90,000 in November when he won his first tournament, a Grand Prix event in Brazil. When he had turned pro in 1986, the computerized tennis rankings rated him only the 403rd player in the world. By the end of 1987, he was 25th.

Even though he was still only seventeen, Andre seemed well on his way to becoming one of the game's top players. Fans wondered if he would take over the top ranking from superstars like Connors, Boris Becker, and Ivan Lendl.

Chapter 5

Agassi Becomes a Star

In 1988 Andre Agassi turned eighteen. This was also the year he officially became one of the best tennis players in the world.

After winning a close three-set match from Agassi in California, Boris Becker wrapped his arm around his young opponent and joked, "I hope you don't get any better."[1]

Andre made it to the semifinals of the French Open and U.S. Open, two of the four Grand Slam events on the professional tour. Even though he lost those matches, he had surprised many fans and players just by making it that far. They seemed to be waiting for him to lose his concentration or just to play bad tennis. That was the old Andre. Now he was confident and calm.

During 1988, he won six tournaments, only losing eleven matches the entire year. Tennis was beginning to make him a very rich young man. From his tournaments that year, he won $822,000. *Tennis* magazine honored him as the 1988's Most Improved Pro. By the end of the year, his ranking had jumped from 25th to 3rd.

Of course, Andre's behavior still wasn't always perfect. Near the end of a match with Martin Jaite, he yelled to Bollettieri, "Watch this." Then, instead of trying to return his opponent's serve, he reached

STATS

1988 End of the Year Rankings

1. Mats Wilander
2. Ivan Lendl
3. Andre Agassi
4. Boris Becker
5. Stefan Edberg
6. Kent Carlsson
7. Jimmy Connors
8. Jakob Hlasek
9. Henri Leconte
10. Tim Mayotte

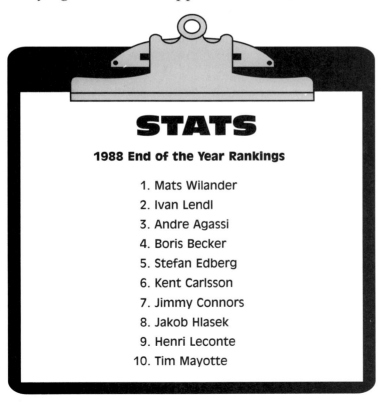

forward and caught it. That gesture and the big smile on his face were supposed to show the crowd that Jaite was a weak server, but instead of laughing, the crowd booed and whistled. Agassi looked like a jerk trying to show up another player. Once again John McEnroe was not impressed. "Andre's young and naive, but that was unbelievable."[2] Even his mother was mad. After the match, she called him from her home in Las Vegas and told him to behave.

Agassi was becoming more than just a winning tennis player. The young athlete had become an exciting superstar. "I can't help but think that Andre's too good to be true," said an agent. "He's so exactly what tennis had been starved for that it's almost as if they invented him to fill a need."[3]

There had always been plenty of great men's tennis players, but by the late 1980s, the fans seemed to be looking for somebody new to cheer for. By then, many aging stars, like Bjorn Borg and Jimmy Connors, had begun to fade or even retire from the game. Other stars played great tennis, but were never very popular. McEnroe's whiny complaints and bad manners on the court kept him from being a favorite with many fans. They weren't fond of Ivan Lendl, either, the No. 1 player who never seemed to smile.

Then along came Agassi. He was young and

handsome, with a wild head of hair. He didn't look like anybody else—and he didn't act like anybody else, either. When he made a good shot, he blew kisses to his fans. When he won a match, he threw a towel, a sweaty shirt, or even an extra pair of tennis shorts into the crowd. When his opponent made a good shot, he smiled and applauded. The spectators could sense that he loved playing the game. "I want tennis to be fun," he said. "I want to enjoy the game, and I am."[4]

Of course, besides being an exciting, likable player, Andre was also a very good one. He wasn't just dressing well and looking cute. He was also charging around the court and making a lot of great shots.

All of a sudden, agents and advertising executives began comparing the eighteen-year-old to basketball superstar Michael Jordan, the man who would one day be earning $40 million a year endorsing everything from shoes to hamburgers. "He's one of only a handful of athletes whose appeal transcends sports," said Ian Hamilton, a Nike executive. "Right now Andre is the hottest endorsement in sports, period."[5]

Nike, which two years before had helped launch Agassi's pro career with a $25,000 contract, now offered him a new one that would pay more than $500,000 a year. Andre accepted that contract and signed another with Donnay Racquets, worth

Everything that Agassi does is watched closely. When he first showed up for a match wearing a cap people asked why. The answer seemed obvious: because the sun was bright.

$1 million a year for the next six years. He was also paid to endorse CoolMax tennis clothes, Ebel watches, Rayban sunglasses, and Canon cameras.

In 1989 all the contracts meant Agassi would make $2.5 million from endorsements alone. That was three times as much as he earned from playing tennis the year before. The deals also meant that he would be earning much more than the other players, even those who were winning more matches and tournaments.

Andre's television commercials and print advertisements were unlike those of other professional athletes. He had a wild, exciting attitude, and so did his endorsements. The first Donnay magazine ads featured a full-page shot of the back of his head. One look at the long, shaggy hair, and tennis fans everywhere knew who was using the racket.

On television, he smashed the ball, then smiled for Nike, twirled his racket, and said, "That ought to wake up the country club." Viewers recognized immediately that Andre wasn't a boring player who dressed in white and played quiet games at country clubs. He was a dangerous, exciting athlete who slashed the ball, got sweaty, and looked like a rock star.

For Canon, Agassi raced back and forth, striking poses for the cameras. The message was simple: "Image is everything." The commercial irritated many

FACT

Unlike basketball or football stars, tennis players do not sign contracts with teams. They earn their money from tournament winnings and appearance fees. The longer a player lasts in a tournament, the more money he makes. Some popular stars are guaranteed a fee just for showing up to play. Most stars also have endorsement contracts with companies that make tennis equipment, shoes, and clothes.

Many businesses wanted Agassi to help advertise their products. One commercial for Donnay Racquets just showed the back of his head. Even still, everyone knew who it was immediately.

reporters, players, and fans. He seemed to be saying that what he accomplished wasn't important, only the way he acted and looked. That was an odd message for an athlete who was trying to win championships.

In order to silence his detractors, Andre had to keep winning. How could they complain about his style and all the money he was making from endorsements if he could still deliver the goods on the tennis court?

Then, in 1989, he seemed to run out of steam. Too many of his matches went like his third-round meeting with Jim Courier at the French Open. In all their years at the academy (sometimes even as roommates) and as pros, Courier had only beaten Agassi once. In fact, he was still looking for his first important tournament victory. By then, he had only earned a No. 47 ranking.

In Paris, the fans cheered for Andre and didn't even seem to notice his opponent, but Courier won the first set 7–6 by taking a 9–7 tie breaker. Agassi won the next set 6–4, then Courier jumped to a 4–2 lead in the third before the match had to be postponed because of darkness.

The next afternoon Agassi tried to regain control, but, as Courier said, "When Andre turned it back on, I turned it back on, too."[6] It took him just forty-four minutes to finish the third set, 6–3, then the fourth, 6–2, for the match. As Courier celebrated, more than a few fans wondered about Agassi: If he was so great, why had he been beaten by the No. 47 player?

Over the next few months, even Andre's racket gave him trouble. Because of the big contract, he had switched from Prince to Donnay. Unfortunately, the handle on his Donnay models just didn't feel right. It twisted in his hand when he hit the ball. His dad, Mike, flew to the Donnay offices in Belgium to attempt to get the problem corrected. For a while, Andre went back to his familiar Prince rackets, but before walking onto the court, stenciled a big D on the strings so they would look like Donnay models. The company finally produced a handle that satisfied Agassi, and he began using their rackets again.

Jim Courier was one of Agassi's classmates at the Nick Bollettieri Tennis Academy. When Courier beat Agassi in the third round of the 1989 French Open he was ranked 47th in the world. Courier eventually reached the No. 1 ranking.

No matter which racket he was using, Andre won just one tournament in 1989. In December, he would have lost a match to the thirty-seven-year-old Connors if the aging star hadn't had to quit because of an injury. "I didn't want to be motivated," Andre said. "I didn't want to come back the next day if I won. I was just fried."[7] The young man who had been playing tennis since he was a baby seemed to have had enough of the sport. "I got really drained at the end of the year [1988] because I played so much tennis. I wasn't prepared for anything anymore—or even where I was. There was a lot of pressure and expectations I put on myself. I had a lot of growing up to do."[8]

Some tennis observers who had never liked Andre's flashy style were quick to suggest that his problem was that he just wasn't a very good player. "Agassi shot to the top by beating outclassed guys," said a veteran player. "But the great players get even better when they play other great players, and he hasn't shown he has that quality."[9]

After almost losing the match to Connors, he decided it was time to try a new approach, so for seven and a half weeks, "Andre cut down on his tennis," said his new trainer, Pat Etcheberry. "I think that break from the court helped him mentally. He's a new man."[10]

The trainer decided that Andre needed to begin

FACT

To take a set, a player must be the first to win six games, but he must win by at least two. If the set score is tied at six games apiece, there's a tiebreaker. The first player to get seven points wins the set—as long as he's at least two points ahead.

cross training. Instead of just playing hour after hour of tennis, he would spend more of his time exercising to stay in shape. Maybe the different workouts would help him be a tougher, stronger competitor. If he spent more time off the court, maybe he could begin to enjoy tennis again.

Etcheberry's training routine was unique. Twice a week they headed for the beach, where he'd pretend to hit shots. Standing barefoot on the sand and without a racket, Andre took off after the imaginary shots. Over and over, he practiced his moves to the left and the right. Then the trainer attached a harness to Andre's back and shoulders, and had the star drag him around the sand. Twice a week, Andre practiced jumping on a hard surface in his tennis shoes. The drills were designed to produce quick bursts of speed.

Andre also began regular vigorous weight lifting workouts with Gil Reyes, a strength and conditioning coach at the University of Nevada at Las Vegas (UNLV) near his home. Soon Reyes gave up his job to travel with Agassi and his brother, Phillip, on the professional tour.

The workouts and the time off the courts seemed to be just what Agassi needed. "I don't know where my potential is," he said early in 1990. "But I hope to find out by giving it my best shot—and knowing that every time I go out there, I'll be a little bit better."[11]

Chapter 6

Ups and Downs

Long, hard workouts seemed to be just what Andre Agassi needed. By the fall of 1990, he had gained twenty pounds of muscle in his arms, legs, and chest. He looked like a new man. Reporters joked that his new nickname should be "Andre the Giant."[1]

Gil Reyes had devised the weight lifting program that enabled Agassi to bulk up. "A year ago I would not have been able to lift 135 pounds one or two times," Andre said. "[Now] I lifted 245 pounds three times."[2] After months of working together, the two had become very good friends. Reyes continued to travel from tournament to tournament with Andre and his brother, Phillip.

When he competed in the 1990 French Open, Agassi wanted to erase the memory of his embarrassing defeat at the hands of Jim Courier a year before. Through the early rounds, he played very well, earning a spot in the quarterfinals against Michael Chang, the 1989 champion.

For the first two sets, Andre was the terror of the Paris clay court, winning 6–2, 6–1. After Chang won 6–4, Agassi ended the match with a decisive 6–2 final set victory.

Then, after beating Jonas Svennson, he was in the final against Andres Gomez. Neither player had ever won a Grand Slam tournament. They split the first two sets, but then Gomez took Agassi apart 6–4, 6–4, and the championship was his. Andre was disappointed, but he hoped he would have plenty of other chances to win a Grand Slam event.

He figured the U.S. Open would be his chance. Once again, he played fine tennis, making it to the semifinals against Boris Becker. The German star was tough; he hung on to take a 7–6 first set win with a 12–10 tiebreaker. Andre refused to get discouraged or give up, though. He kept pounding the ball past Becker from the baseline. The match quickly ended with three Agassi set victories, 6–3, 6–2, 6–3.

In the final, he would meet Pete Sampras, a nineteen-year-old American who had never won a Grand Slam event. Sampras had never before even made it to the finals of a major tournament. He had a blistering serve, however, that had already begun to give fits to many of the veteran players. It wasn't unusual for them to explode over the net at speeds approaching 130 miles per hour.

Against Agassi, Sampras's serve was right on target again and again. Andre had a reputation as a man who could return serves better than almost anybody in the game, but he couldn't handle the bullets that kept coming. The match was a quick, easy win for Sampras, 6–4, 6–3, 6–2.

Agassi continued to win most of his matches and even a few minor tournaments, but fans were still wondering if he would ever be able to win a Grand Slam title. There was nothing for him to do but keep plugging away, practicing, playing, and hoping that the next time he made it to a major final, he'd get the job done.

Late in the year, Agassi, Sampras, Becker, Ivan Lendl, and Stefan Edberg traveled to Frankfurt, Germany, for the 1990 ATP Tour World Championship. It was a round-robin tournament, not a single-elimination event. A player could lose a match, but still come back to win the championship. To win a match (except in the final), he would only have to take two sets, not the usual three.

When Agassi met Sampras, the players and the fans couldn't help remembering the thrashing he'd been given at the U.S. Open. Andre was ready to play and anxious for revenge. He quickly trounced

FACT

A player wins the Grand Slam by taking all four major tournaments in one year. Only two men have ever accomplished the feat—Don Budge in 1938 and Rod Laver in 1962 and 1969. For the women, Maureen Connolly (1953), Margaret Smith Court (1970) and Steffi Graf (1988) have all won Grand Slams.

Sampras 6–4, 6–2. "I was out to prove that the Open was just one day in New York," he said.[3]

When he lost a heartbreaking 7–6, 4–6, 7–6 decision to Edberg, he didn't lose his focus. He came right back to destroy Becker 6–2, 6–4, to earn a spot in the final.

Once again he would be facing Edberg, the world's No. 1 player, who had already beaten him once in the tournament as well as whipping Sampras and Lendl in straight sets. It would be a very tough match for Andre in an important final. Many reporters and fans figured Edberg was almost a sure winner.

After Agassi lost a tough 7–5 first set, the crowd wondered how he would respond. Would he give up? Would he choke? Not this time. With the pressure on, he fought Edberg to a 6–6 tie, paving the way for the tiebreaker. Then the pressure was really on, but he coolly took it, 7–5. After Agassi won the third set, 7–5, Edberg faded. Andre won the finale, 6–2, and the title.

The ATP Tour World Championship wasn't a Grand Slam event, but it was a very important tournament against the best players in the world. Andre earned $950,000, in his biggest payday yet. It was the high point of his professional career. "I feel as good about winning here,"—he smiled—, "as I felt bad about losing two Grand Slam finals."[4]

FACT

Tennis is one of the few sports that expects fans to remain silent when a game is about to begin. Serving players do not want to be distracted by talking or moving in the stands. Once the serve is made, however, spectators may yell and cheer. Booing is seldom heard; fans who disagree with a call usually whistle.

Then Andre led the American team to victory in the finals of the Davis Cup competition against Australia. It was the first U.S. win in eight years. After defeating Richard Fromberg in five sets, he was so happy he couldn't help boasting, "I didn't win it with tennis. It was something else—just guts."[5]

As usual, Andre's popularity didn't seem to depend much on his performance on the courts. Because of his style and the excitement that always seemed to surround him, he was almost always the crowd's favorite. Even people who didn't know much about tennis could recognize him and the products he endorsed. No matter what he was doing with his rackets, the money kept pouring in from his contracts—especially the big ones with Nike and Donnay. He was still earning much more money from endorsements than from his tennis.

Andre was starting to enjoy his millions. He began buying cars for his friends and himself. Included in his collection were several Cadillacs, a Ferrari, and a Lamborghini. At his new home in Las Vegas, one room was entirely devoted to his favorite video arcade games. He had his own built-in soda machine, a swimming lagoon, and a sauna.

During the first part of 1991, Agassi continued to play steady tennis. By the time of the French Open in

FACT

Since 1900, teams from around the world have competed for the Davis Cup. When two teams meet, they play four singles matches and one doubles match. Today the country that stays undefeated through the tournament of sixteen nations is crowned the world champion of men's tennis.

June, he was ranked No. 4. Once again he fought his way into the finals. His opponent would be Courier.

The two Americans in their baseball caps blasted away at each other for hours on the French clay. Finally, the fifth and deciding set was tied 4–4. Even though he was serving, Andre fell behind 15–40.

On the next point, after a long rally, Courier popped up a lob. It was supposed to go over Agassi, driving him behind the baseline for the return. Then Courier could slice a winner past him, but the lob was short, very short. After the ball bounced, it hung in the air, waiting to be smashed back for an easy point. Andre took a powerful swing, but the ball went out of bounds. Instead of being back in the game, he had lost the point and his serve.

Courier quickly won his own service, and the match was over. Agassi had lost his third consecutive Grand Slam final. His eyes were filled with tears when he said, "The pessimistic side of me questions if I'll ever win one."[6]

A few months later, his worst fears seemed to be realized when he was knocked out of the U.S. Open in the first round. For a while he thought again about giving up tennis. Maybe he just wasn't cut out to be a tennis champion. He traveled to the University of Arizona, where his friend Perry Rogers was attending law school. His old friend

FACT

Jim Courier's victory over Andre Agassi in the 1991 French Open was his first Grand Slam championship. Since then he has won three more—the French Open again in 1992 and the Australian Open in 1992 and 1993. He lost in the finals of the 1993 Wimbledon tournament to Pete Sampras.

Fully extended, Andre looks to hit a backhand winner. Agassi met Jim Courier in the 1991 French Open final. Courier won the title.

asked an important question: "Do you like tennis?" Andre was surprised and could only answer, "I don't know."[7] If he wasn't going to be a tennis player, what could he be?

Agassi finally decided that he still wasn't ready to give up his sport. After years of practice, he was hardly ready to quit. His improved strength and his victories in the Davis Cup and the ATP Tour Championship gave him hope that someday he was going to win a Grand Slam title. He was still young, and he still had a lot of tennis left to play.

Almost everybody had forgotten the prediction he had made in 1990 about his conditioning and weight lifting. "I'm really preparing myself for 1992, when I'll be ready to go big time."[8]

Chapter 7

From Ecstasy to Injury

Andre Agassi was right. Winning the 1992 Wimbledon championship made him a big-time, respected tennis star. Millions of fans watched as he fell to his knees and sobbed after defeating Goran Ivanisevic 6–7, 6–4, 6–4, 1–6, 6–4. It was an incredible match and a magnificent victory. "Any time you go five sets fighting so hard to kill each other, you have so much respect," he said. "You have to be an athlete."[1]

Finally, Agassi had the respect of the tennis world. Now he had the grandest Grand Slam trophy of them all, to go with all the millions of dollars he was already earning. The only person who didn't seem impressed was his father, Mike, the man who had put a racket in his hand when he was still wearing diapers. After the Wimbledon final, Mike didn't want to talk about the victory. He wanted to tell Andre about the mistakes he had made that cost him the fourth set.

Agassi tried to not be bothered by his father's attitude. He was very proud of his Wimbledon championship, and he enjoyed the respect he had earned from the reporters, fans, and the other players. Finally, he had shown that he wasn't just a hotshot with a cute smile, a radical haircut, and a strange wardrobe.

Besides being cool, Andre was also very rich. His advertisements for cameras, rackets, and clothes earned him millions of dollars a year. It seemed strange that he was making much more money from his endorsement contracts than stars like Ivan Lendl, John McEnroe, Stefan Edberg, and Boris Becker, each of whom had won several Grand Slam tournaments. "Most people have to work really hard and win some big matches, and then they get money and popularity," Andre admitted. "For me it has been the reverse of everybody else. The exact opposite."[2]

FACT

Since World War II, only two Americans—John McEnroe and Pete Sampras—have won three Wimbledon championships. McEnroe took the title in 1981, 1983, and 1984, while Sampras won in 1993, 1994, and 1995. Jimmy Connors, another American, has two championships, in 1974 and 1982.

Not everybody liked Agassi. Mr. Blackwell, a fashion critic, said he dressed like "an outdated flower child." Blackwell believed Andre "has every right to wear whatever he wants to wear, provided he has some respect for the sport he's in. Let him wear his neon, flower-child-gone-to-seed shorts. But

I would suggest he get himself in front of a mirror before he goes out in public."[3]

Ivan Lendl, one of the world's best tennis players, was disgusted by Agassi's popularity. "I'm sad anyone can cherish Andre. The kids see him as a rebel with his earring, hair and no-shave look."[4]

Nobody argued that Agassi was not a very talented athlete, but many felt that he didn't take his talent seriously enough. While other players worked hard every minute they were on the court, he sometimes seemed to give up if he fell behind. While others chose their diets carefully, he seemed to survive on candy, hamburgers, and soda. While others waved calmly to the crowd after a victory, he threw towels and shorts to his fans. While others chose their words carefully when speaking to reporters, Andre seemed to say whatever popped into his head. As he himself admitted, "I have an uncanny ability to make people think I'm stupid."[5]

Andre continued to enjoy his money. He bought his own private jet so he could fly in comfort on his own schedule from tournament to tournament. On its tail was painted a big A crossed by a flying tennis ball.

Over the next year, however, the jet spent a surprising amount of time on the ground, because often Andre wasn't going anywhere. Early in the year, he won tournaments in San Francisco and

Arizona, but then injuries and illnesses forced him to the sidelines. He cut back to only thirteen tournaments in the twelve months after Wimbledon. He couldn't play in the 1993 Australian Open, because he had bronchitis. He had to sit out the French Open because of tendinitis in his right wrist.

When he was finally able to enter a minor tournament in Halle, Germany, just before Wimbledon, he was knocked out in the first round by Carl-Uwe Steeb, the world's No. 58 player.

His wrist hurt so badly that he wondered if he would even be able to defend his Wimbledon title. He couldn't do a push-up or shoot a basketball. To help the wrist heal, he received injections of cortisone from his doctors. The shots eased the pain, but they also caused his body to swell.

When Agassi arrived at Wimbledon, he was a popular but strange-looking figure. His picture was splashed all over the London newspapers, and screaming British fans followed him everywhere. More than fans in any other country, they almost all seemed to enjoy Andre. "They love to have me," he said, "and I love to be here."[6]

Unfortunately, he looked fat and out of shape. He admitted that in the month before the tournament, he had only been able to play about an hour of tennis. Apparently, he had gotten very little other exercise,

FACT

Ivan Lendl and Jimmy Connors have spent more weeks atop the mens rankings than any other player. Lendl was number one for 270 weeks in the 1980s and 1990s. Connors, who played his best tennis in the 1970s, had 268 weeks on top.

either, because he now had a chubby belly that hung over the top of his shorts. His weight trainer, Gil Reyes, claimed that his bloated appearance was entirely due to the effects of the cortisone.

At first the biggest story in the London papers was not Andre's belly or his tennis ability, but his chest. When he changed shirts during an early match, fans and photographers noticed that all the hair on his chest was gone. "It makes me a little more aerodynamic out there," he explained.[7]

Then Barbra Streisand, a singer, actress, and director who was probably even more famous than Andre, showed up to root for him. Suddenly reporters forgot about the missing chest hair and began writing stories about a possible romance between the two stars. Their friendship attracted a good deal of attention, because the fifty-one-year-old Streisand was twenty-eight years older than the tennis player. Before Andre was even born, Streisand had already won an Academy Award for her acting.

With all the articles being written about his belly, chest, wrist, and friend, many reporters seemed to have forgotten about the tennis tournament. They hardly seemed to notice his competition on the court.

When Andre met Pete Sampras in the quarterfinals, Streisand was in the stands waving and

FACT

Sports writers and coaches rank college teams in basketball and hockey. It's a simple system: they just vote for the team they think is best. The team with the most votes is number one. Rankings for the top professional tennis players are done differently. They are ranked by the ATP Tour computer on a scale that takes into account tournament victories and defeats.

After winning the 1992 Wimbledon championship, Agassi suffered a wrist injury that severely limited his ability to play and practice. When he returned for the 1993 Wimbledon tournament he was not in top form.

cheering. The television cameras kept focusing on his famous friend. Meanwhile, Sampras wasn't thinking about his girlfriend or his hair. He was concentrating on his tennis, and he won the first two sets easily 6–2, 6–2.

Agassi managed to win the next two sets 6–3, 6–3, but then Sampras took the deciding fifth set 6–4. Andre and Barbra then disappeared from Wimbledon. Pete stuck around, beating Boris Becker in the semis and Jim Courier in the final. It was his first Grand Slam victory since he'd whipped Agassi in the 1990 U.S. Open final.

When it was over, Sampras said he was puzzled by Andre. "He's got so many distractions. Everywhere he goes he's mobbed. Maybe he causes it. Maybe he likes it. I don't know."[8]

Soon after Wimbledon, Nick Bollettieri, his coach for ten years, decided he had had enough. He wrote Andre a letter, telling him he wasn't interested in working with him anymore. "Nick hurt me," Agassi said. "When things like that happen, it can make you lose hope in people."[9]

Of course, not everybody blamed Bollettieri. "Andre's a guy who's never really given everything he's got to the game," said Jim Courier. "He'll give most of what he's got, for a while. Then he'll stop. Then he'll get fat."[10]

Agassi was losing much of the respect he had gained from his 1992 victory. If he wanted to be taken seriously as a tennis player, he would have to get back in shape and win some tournaments. Then pain in his wrist injury forced him to take some time off. In December 1993, doctors operated to remove scar tissue.

Overcome with emotion, Agassi throws his hands in the air to celebrate a win. Unfortunately for Agassi, his wrist injury and eventual surgery gave him little to cheer about in 1993.

As he rested and waited impatiently for his wrist to heal, Agassi knew his future in tennis was in doubt. Many people doubted that he would ever compete again. Without exercise, he had gained eight more pounds. Even if his wrist healed, how long would it take him to get back in shape? Would he be able to make it without Bollettieri? Was he even willing to give up silly stunts like shaving his chest and concentrate on practicing and playing serious tennis?

Agassi had to do some serious thinking. He knew that many reporters and players had begun to suspect that the Wimbledon victory was a fluke. They didn't think he was mature enough to get his act together. They figured he was satisfied with being a clown.

Andre thought a lot about how his father had pushed him into the sport. He remembered how hard Nick Bollettieri had made him work. He couldn't forget all the thousands of hours he had already invested in the sport in practices and competitions. He had to be sure that he wanted to play tennis and win, not for his father or Bollettieri, but for himself.

He discussed his future with many friends, including Streisand, who was trying to make a big decision of her own. Despite selling millions of records, she hadn't appeared in a concert tour since before Andre was born. She had kept herself busy with movies, and, besides, she didn't really like performing live. She had millions of fans, but she also had stage fright. Over the years, she had turned down millions of dollars in performance contracts because she was afraid to again sing in public.

Andre took time out from pondering his own future to convince Streisand to return to the stage. According to one source, he "impressed upon Barbra that her gifts as a singer needed to be shared with others."[11] She signed a multimillion-dollar contract for two concerts in Las Vegas, Agassi's hometown.

As Streisand began rehearsals, Agassi began making plans to share his own enormous gifts as an athlete with his own fans. When he came back, he would have a new coach and a new girlfriend, and he would be ready.

Chapter 8

The Road Back

While Andre Agassi recuperated from wrist surgery, his ranking fell to No. 32.

Agassi and the doctors weren't even sure he would ever be able to play again. What if the pain was still there? What if the weakened wrist couldn't be strengthened by therapy and exercise? "The surgery had a direct impact on my tennis because I had to deal with the possibility of not playing."[1]

While he rested, he thought about his family, his friends, and his future. "I feel like when you work on yourself and you strive to understand, then you get to a place where things start to become healthy."[2]

And, of course, he thought about the way he would approach his sport if and when he could get back on the court. "I do feel a responsibility to my ability, and that's in my preparation and my practice habits and my training habits and my strategy and preparation for each match. These are things I can control. The way that ball bounces, some days, I can't control."[3]

Andre resolved that he was going to be a calmer, happier person who would enjoy life. When he was healthy, he was going to work harder than ever to become a tougher, more consistent competitor.

Early in 1994, Agassi's wrist healed, and he was back on the court. The pain was gone, and he could hit the ball as hard as ever. "When I'm out there I'm loving it and I'm enjoying it. That's something I thank God for every day. It's not right to have a gift and not go out there and just enjoy it."[4]

In March, he hired a new coach—Brad Gilbert, a former player with years of experience. Together, they planned the training program and strategies he would use when he returned to the court. Gilbert convinced him that he wasn't using his head when he played. Andre didn't always think about his shots, and he liked to spend almost all his time whacking balls from the baseline. His opponents were hardly ever surprised by what he did. Sure, the coach said, it was great to have talent, but Andre had to learn to vary his shots.[5]

By now, he also had a new girlfriend, Brooke

FACT

The ATP Tour rankings count only a player's best fourteen tournaments during the past fifty-two weeks. This has led to some controversy, especially after Thomas Muster became No. 1. The German star usually does poorly when he plays on any surface except clay. Those early-round losses on hard court and grass are not counted because of his many clay victories.

Shields, a stage and movie actress who was five years older than Agassi. On their first date at a Los Angeles restaurant, the waitress, standing behind him and noticing just his long hair, asked, "Are you ladies enjoying your meal?"[6]

They had gotten to know each other by fax while Shields was in Australia and Africa shooting two movies. Andre stayed home in the United States, but they communicated—over and over—by fax. Her first was a funny note she had written because she was bored, but Andre sent back a long sweet message, and then, he said, "She wrote back a novel."[7]

Shields was especially impressed by Agassi when she had an operation of her own. After doctors removed bunions on her feet, she said she was "alone and unattractive." Andre didn't just send a card or flowers; he came to New York City to be with her. "Even when I looked my worst and was puking," she said, "he never left my side."[8]

From then on, when she wasn't shooting a movie or appearing on Broadway, Shields could usually be found in the stands cheering and taking photographs while Agassi played. She also spent some time with his parents. "Isn't she wonderful?" Andre asked. As usual, it was hard for his father, Mike, to think of anything pleasant. "She's too tall," was all he could say.[9]

Agassi was a happy man and an improving tennis player. In March 1994, he made it to the final of the Lipton Championships in Key Biscayne, Florida. When Pete Sampras was too sick to start playing on time, Andre could have taken a victory by default. Instead, he gave Sampras time to see a doctor and recover. It was a classy move, and Sampras appreciated it, but that didn't stop him from whipping Andre, 5–7, 6–3, 6–3, for the title.

At Wimbledon in June 1994, he fared even worse. Even with Shields in the stands, and with no more

When Agassi returned to the tennis court in 1994, he was dating actress Brooke Shields. Soon Shields could be seen at Agassi's matches cheering him on.

Planting his foot, Agassi prepares to smash a forehand winner. With his wrist fully healed, Agassi started to come back with a vengeance in the summer of 1994.

silly stunts like a chest shave, he was knocked out in the fourth round.

The next Grand Slam tournament was the U.S. Open held in New York City during the final weeks of summer. Nobody really expected Agassi to be a factor; he was seeded No. 20. That meant the organizers figured there were nineteen better players in the tournament.

Andre didn't care what anybody else thought. "When I step on the court I feel like I'm going to win the match and that's not going to change, whatever number is next to my name."[10] He won enough matches to earn a spot in the quarterfinals against Thomas Muster.

Agassi took a tiebreaker to win the first set. "The more he got confident, the better he played," Muster said. Andre won the last two sets 6–3, 6–0. "He played harder than me," his opponent said. "Everything I did, he did better."[11]

Agassi's confidence grew. As he looked over Stadium Court, packed with loudly cheering fans, he said, "I feel like it's my arena."[12] In the semifinals, he split the first two sets with Todd Martin 6–3, 4–6. "I played a flash of good tennis in the second set and he didn't let that bother him," Martin said. "This guy is a superstar. He can dress up in goofy clothes on TV and make commercials and people still like him."[13]

All of a sudden, Agassi was back in a Grand Slam final, his first since his victory two years earlier at Wimbledon. Reporters kept reminding their readers about the last time he had made it this far in the U.S. Open. Four years before, Sampras had taken him apart in straight sets.

As he stood waiting to walk onto Stadium Court, Andre vowed that his finals match with Michael Stich would be different. His body was shaking in anticipation, but he wasn't scared. He just couldn't wait to start playing. "There's no way this guy's coming here and taking my title," he told Brad Gilbert.[14]

His coach was sure he was ready. Now, he felt, Andre was truly a great player, not just an athlete who could really bash a tennis ball. He was confident that Agassi would surprise Stich with his shots and his strategy.

When the match began, he looked comfortable slapping shots over the net from his customary spot near the baseline, but he refused to stay there. Soon he was charging the net, forcing Stich to retreat behind his own baseline. When the six-foot-four-inch German star rushed the net, Agassi sent beautiful lobs sailing over his head.

After the match, Andre used golfing terms to explain what he'd been doing on Stadium Court. "You can't play strong and be mentally weak; you

FACT

Tennis opponents take turns serving. When a player is serving, he is usually expected to win. If the serving player loses, it's a service *break* and he's at a big disadvantage because in order to win the set, he now must get a service break of his own.

Michael Stich was Agassi's opponent in the 1994 U.S. Open Final. Stich had been the Wimbledon champion in 1991.

have to put it all together or else it's like hitting the green and not sinking the putts."[15]

In the first set, he broke Stich three times. Each time Andre made an especially good shot, he held up his hands and looked toward the spot in the stands where Shields sat with his parents. Finally, Stich double-faulted in the seventh game, and Agassi had a 6–1 set victory. The set had only taken twenty-four minutes.

The second set was longer and closer; finally it came down to a tiebreak. A vicious backhand return by Agassi exploded the ball back at Stich's feet and put him ahead 4–2. Four shots later, Andre jammed Stich with a serve that bounced up close to his backhand. The return hit the net, and Agassi was up by two sets.

The third set was another close one as the players fought their way to a 5–5 tie. Then Andre's awesome power turned the tide. He blasted a backhand bullet straight at Stich, who couldn't hit it or even get out of the way. The ball bounced off his wrist. Agassi apologized for accidentally hitting his opponent, but then smashed a forehand volley right back at him. This time Stich was quick enough to get his racket on the ball, but the shot popped out of bounds. Soon Andre was up 6–5, and serving for the match.

He won the first three points, then forced Stich to

Agassi celebrates a tournament win by showing the trophy to his adoring fans. Agassi won his second Grand Slam event by beating Michael Stich for the U.S. Open title in 1994.

chase a shot near the sidelines, leaving the court open for an easy backhand winner. Agassi had won the U.S. Open title in straight sets 6–1, 7–6, 7–5!

In a repeat of his emotional celebration at Wimbledon, Andre fell to the hard court on his knees while Shields and his parents rose to cheer his victory. Stich walked around the net and helped his victorious opponent to his feet. The two men embraced, then Andre raced to the stands to kiss Shields.

He was so happy after getting his trophy that all he could tell a TV interviewer was "But uh wow!"[16]

It felt great to be the winner of his second Grand Slam event, but Agassi and his coach were soon establishing new goals. That day at Stadium Court Gilbert told him, "You're going to win the Australian Open."[17]

Andre wanted more than just a few more major titles. He told reporters, "I can be the best player in the world."[18]

Chapter 9

Number One Player

By the end of 1994, Andre Agassi was moving up the tennis rankings, setting his sights on the No. 1 player, Pete Sampras. It was almost time to go to Australia for that country's Grand Slam tournament.

Before leaving the United States, Andre had decided there was something he wanted to do. There was a hairstylist waiting for him in Brooke Shields's New York City apartment.

Andre nervously sat down, and the stylist lifted up his famous ponytail. Snip! The ponytail was gone! Within a few minutes, almost all his hair was gone. In place of the long, shaggy brown hair was a short buzz cut. "That feels weird," he said.[1]

Leaping high into the air, Agassi delivers a forehand smash. In late 1994, Agassi decided to trade in his long flowing hair for a new buzz cut.

Why did he want to change his look? His hair had become famous around the world. Had he lost a bet? Did the Nike company ask him to do it? Was he just looking for more publicity?

The answer, he said, was simple. Just like his brother, Phillip, Andre was losing his hair. A long hairstyle, he finally decided, would look kind of silly when the top of his head would soon be bald. Unlike Phillip, he didn't want to bother with a hair weave or a wig. It would be easier just to cut almost all of it off.

The fans in Australia went wild when he showed up without his trademark ponytail. "Brooke loves it," he told them. "I just felt myself so free, like I don't have to worry about not being able to get ready in ten minutes."[2]

In the tournament itself, much attention was focused on the classy courage of Sampras. Just before an early match, his coach and friend, Tim Gullikson, was rushed to the hospital. Within days, he was flown back to the United States, where he was diagnosed with brain cancer. "It just broke my heart," Sampras said.[3] During a changeover break in his quarterfinal match with Jim Courier, he said, "I started thinking about Tim, and I just broke down."[4] At first he tried to hide his tears by pretending to wipe away sweat on his face with his sleeve. Soon he was sobbing into a towel. Courier offered to continue the match the next day, but Sampras bravely got up and won a five-set thriller. Then he whipped Michael Chang to earn a spot in the final.

Meanwhile, Agassi was overwhelming his opponents. It wasn't until he met Sampras in the final that he finally lost his first set of the tournament. Despite serving with tears in his eyes, Sampras was magnificent in a 6–4 set victory.

Then Andre battled back to win two sets, 6–1 and 7–6. Sampras hoped that his vicious serve could bring him back into the match, but Agassi hung tough and slugged back return after return. Finally Andre took the title 6–4.

After the match, Sampras talked to the crowd about his coach. "I wish he was here. I've been praying for him the last couple of weeks." The Australian Open was Agassi's second Grand Slam victory in a row and one of the highlights of his career, but when he took the microphone, he talked about Sampras. "His courage on the court and off the court is absolutely inspiring," he said. "He's a class act."[5]

Three months later, on April 10, 1995, Agassi achieved his goal of being the best player in the world. According to the official ATP Tour rankings, he took over the No. 1 spot from Sampras, who had been on top since September 13, 1993. He became just the twelfth man to hold the No. 1 spot in twenty-two years since the rankings had been established.

"I think he deserves it," Sampras said. "He's playing very well."[6] Tennis fans—and the players themselves—looked forward to the continuing rivalry between the two superstars. "It is a great high, two heavyweights going at it," Sampras said. "It is something that is great for the game." Andre agreed. "The intensity against Pete is above and beyond anything I can feel with anybody at this time. This is a great stage for tennis."[7]

Agassi was very happy to be the top-ranked player, but, he said, there was something else that mattered more. "It's important for me to be the best that I can."[8]

In his next important match, he collided with Courier in the final of the Japan Open in Tokyo. Courier's serve was on target, and Andre was in trouble. He lost the first set 6-4, and was trailing the second 5-3, facing match point, when Courier lobbed a backhand shot over his head. Agassi raced back and managed to get the ball, but his shot went long. "It's nice to see him playing this well again," he said of his opponent, "but I'm not too excited that it's at my expense."[9]

Andre Agassi beat Pete Sampras to win the 1995 Australian Open. Sampras had won the same tournament in 1994.

At Wimbledon, Andre dropped a semifinal match to Boris Becker after leading 6–2, 4–1. "When it slips away like this, this doesn't feel great," he said, "but you have to take the good with the bad. It's going to happen sooner or later."[10] Sampras then beat Becker for the title, but Agassi retained his No. 1 ranking.

A few weeks later the two top players met in the finals of the Canadian Open in Montreal. In a best two-out-of-three match, they split the first two sets. Andre jumped to a 3–1 lead, but then almost lost his

STATS

Agassi's Grand Slam Championships

Tournament	Year
Wimbledon	1992
U.S. Open	1994, 1999
Australian Open	1995, 2000
French Open	1999

service. He had to fight off three break points. "I was hitting some big, heavy shots on those break points—you have to at that point," he said. "But if you let him make it 4–4, Pete's dangerous." Agassi won the deciding set, 6–3.[11]

Sampras said Andre's serve had become a very potent weapon. "His serve is basically a shot to get you moving his way. And once he gets you going side to side, he's got you."[12] The decision in Montreal evened Sampras's lifetime record against Agassi at eight wins apiece.

At his next tournament, the ATP Championship in Mason, Ohio, a blistering sun and courtside temperatures of 120 degrees convinced Andre to give up the dark bandanna and black shoes and socks he had been wearing for most of the year. He switched to an all-white outfit and dropped Michael Chang 7–5, 6–2, for the title. "I've been playing really well," he said. "I've got myself to the place where I believe I can win every tournament. I get up for the big matches."[13]

By the time the U.S. Open began in August, Agassi had won twenty straight matches. The streak included four straight championships. He had already taken seven tournaments in 1995, his best total ever. As was expected, he met Sampras in the final.

In the opening set, Sampras led 5–4 and had a break point against Agassi. The ball whistled back and forth across the net twenty-two times in one of the most breathtaking rallies of all time. Both men were playing all out, hitting smart, powerful shots. Finally, Sampras cleared the net with a crosscourt winner. After that, he was in command most of the way and took a 6–4, 6–3, 4–6, 7–5 triumph.

Despite losing the U.S. Open, Andre was still No. 1. His success on the court had also earned him more than $2 million in 1995. Of course, that was still almost pocket change compared to the money he continued to make from endorsements. Early in the year, he had signed a new contract with Nike that would pay him $100 million over the next ten years.

Agassi's popularity made him very valuable to the company and to the sport. "The idea is to get people excited about tennis again," said Ian Hamilton, a Nike executive. "And it's working. People are talking about tennis, playing tennis and buying tennis products."[14]

Andre had showed up at the U.S. Open with another new look—baggy black pants, a brown-and-white-striped shirt, and, of course, a bandanna wrapped around his head. As usual, his fans loved

Michael Chang burst onto the tennis scene by winning the 1989 French Open. Agassi was victorious over Chang in winning the 1995 ATP Championship.

his style. "I just want to see if he's going to look like a pirate or a tennis player," one joked.[15]

Nike set up a sales booth near Louis Armstrong Stadium, site of the U.S. Open. "People come here straight from the court and buy whatever they just saw Agassi wearing," said a salesperson. "They just want to look exactly like Andre."[16]

Late in 1995, he signed a new endorsement contract with another giant company. "The 25-year-old tennis phenom is also one of the world's hottest

STATS

In the summer of 1995, Agassi finally rose to the number one spot.

Rank	W	L	Points
1. Andre Agassi	72	8	5400
2. Pete Sampras	55	12	4959
3. Thomas Muster	76	11	4072
4. Boris Becker	40	14	3420
5. Michael Chang	50	14	3015

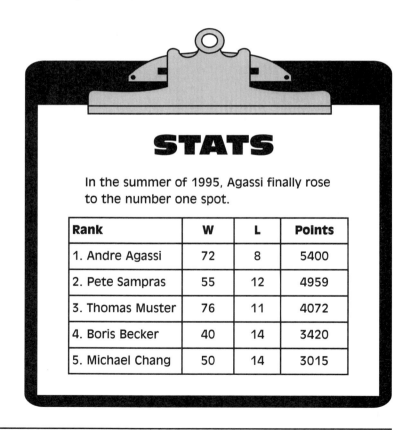

sports marketing properties," said a spokesperson for Pepsi-Cola. "His aggressive style, radical on-court dress and edgy attitude have made him one of the most popular sports celebrities in the world today."[17] For at least two years, Andre would appear in advertisements for Mountain Dew in the United States and for Pepsi Max, a diet drink, in fifty other countries.

Moving across the court, Andre tries to get to his opponent's volley. Agassi showed up at the 1995 U.S. Open with a new look: black sneakers and a brown striped shirt.

In April 1996, construction began on an Official All Star Cafe in Las Vegas. Agassi was partners with Wayne Gretzky, Ken Griffey, Jr., Joe Montana, Shaquille O'Neal, and Monica Seles in the restaurants, which already had sites in New York City and Cancún, Mexico. Andre told reporters he thought sports was a great theme for a restaurant. "I think sports is one area of life that really transcends the entire world. It brings everyone together. You don't need to speak the same language or agree with each other."[18]

To keep track of all the money he keeps making, he has formed Andre Agassi Enterprises, a company with a dozen employees. Its offices are in a Las Vegas bank building. His old friend Perry Rogers is his manager.

Andre bought a city block on the edge of downtown Las Vegas a mile from his home. On the property he built beautiful homes for his parents and for Gil Reyes, his trainer. Behind the houses are a tennis court, health spa, and satellite dishes. When he got tired of his video arcade games, he gave them to Reyes's children.

Even without video games, of course, Agassi continues to have fun. He was very happy when he and the rest of the American team played a Davis Cup match in Las Vegas against Sweden. "It is great to have a chance to play top level tennis in my hometown," he said.[19] Before the match began, he spent more than $40,000 to rent a water park for one night. Wet and Wild was closed to everybody except the two teams and their guests. "There is a certain amount of responsibility I feel to make sure the guys enjoy themselves and get a different look at what it is like to live here."[20]

Andre also felt a responsibility to help disadvantaged young people living in his hometown. He established the Andre Agassi Foundation to fund programs for the youth of Las Vegas. In September 1995, the foundation sponsored a Grand Slam for Children benefit concert. Entertainers like Robin Williams and Elton John helped raise $1.8 million.

While he was in Key Biscayne, Florida, for the Lipton Championships in March 1996, Andre visited with patients from the Children's Cancer Caring

Center. He gave gifts to the kids, signed autographs, then asked them to sign the bandanna he would wear in the opening rounds.

On court at the tournament, he was back in the groove again. "I really feel I'm hitting the ball clean, going for my shots with a lot of confidence."[21]

In the final, Goran Ivanisevic was unable to start on time because of a painfully stiff neck. Andre could have demanded a default and an automatic victory, but he said he would wait while doctors and trainers worked on Ivanisevic. "I'm not here to somehow end up with the trophy," he said. "I'm here to beat the guys who beat the guys."[22]

After forty minutes, Ivanisevic finally tried to play, but he had to quit in the fourth game with Andre leading 3-0. "It was a disappointing way to win the title and for the tournament to end," Agassi said.[23] "It would have been a great match."[24]

In the summer of 1996, he led America's tennis team to the Olympics in Atlanta, Georgia. Andre won the gold medal by defeating Sergi Bruguera, 6–2, 6–3, 6–1, in the championship match.

By then he was no longer the world's No. 1 ranked player. After thirty weeks in the top spot, he had lost it to Sampras in November 1995. In the early months of 1996, the two men had taken turns at No. 1 with Thomas Muster.

FACT

If Andre Agassi had been born a few decades earlier, he wouldn't have gotten rich playing tennis. Until fairly recently, it was an amateur sport and players won only trophies at tournaments. The Grand Slam events were not open to professionals until 1968, two years before Agassi was born.

Since the fall of 1994, Agassi has either been ranked No. 1 or somewhere in the top ten. Agassi hopes his winning ways will continue for a long time to come.

Agassi had perhaps the most disappointing season of his career in 1997. Bothered by injuries, he could only enter twelve tournaments the entire year. In eight of those tournaments he suffered a first round defeat. At the end of 1996 he ranked No. 8 in the world. By the end of 1997, he had fallen to No. 122.

Once again, Andre Agassi was forced to make a comeback. In early 1998, he proved that he could still play with the best of them. By the end of May he had raised his ranking to No. 20 in the world. In 1999, he won both the French and U.S. Opens, and finished the year ranked No. 1. He then won the 2000 Australian Open—the sixth grand slam title of his career.

Agassi remained confident that he would be playing good tennis for years to come. "I have a lot more belief in my game now, and I think you need that, because I'm definitely playing better," he said. "To do what you got to do is the key. The downside is you can't stay on top forever. Eventually, either guys overtake you or you hit a brick wall. I haven't got there yet. But everybody goes through that. I've just got to be able to do it as long as I can."[25]

Chapter Notes

Chapter 1

1. Curry Kirkpatrick, "Agassi and Ecstasy," *Sports Illustrated*, vol. 77, no. 2, July 13, 1992, p. 15.

2. Associated Press dispatch from Wimbledon, England, July 4, 1992.

3. Gannett News Service dispatch from Wimbledon, England, July 5, 1992.

4. Kirkpatrick, p. 16.

5. Gannett, July 5, 1992.

6. Ibid.

7. Ibid.

8. Ibid.

Chapter 2

1. Peter de Jonge, "Born on the Baseline," *New York Times Magazine*, October 30, 1988, p. 44.

2. Ross Wetzsteon, "I Was a Teenage U.S. Hope," *Sport*, vol. 80, no. 7, July 1989, p. 61.

3. Ibid.

4. Sally Jenkins, "Love and Love," *Sports Illustrated*, vol. 82, no. 10, March 13, 1995, p. 57.

5. Nick Bollettieri, "Lethal Weapon," *World Tennis*, vol. 36, no. 7, December 1988, p. 19.

6. Wetzsteon, p. 61.

7. de Jonge, p. 44.

8. Jenkins, p. 56.

9. de Jonge, p. 44.

Chapter 3

1. Gary Stern, *Andre Agassi: Tennis Prince* (Vero Beach, Fla.: Rourke Enterprises, Inc., 1993), p. 15.

2. Andre Agassi, "Rookie on Tour," *World Tennis*, vol. 35, no. 7, December 1987, pp. 36, 50.

3. Peter de Jonge, "Born on the Baseline," *New York Times Magazine*, October 30, 1988, p. 76.

4. Ibid.

5. Ibid.

6. Sally Jenkins, "Love and Love," *Sports Illustrated*, vol. 82, no. 10, March 13, 1995, p. 57.

7. de Jonge, p. 77.

Chapter 4

1. Peter de Jonge, "Born on the Baseline," *New York Times Magazine*, October 30, 1988, p. 42.

2. Andre Agassi, "Rookie on Tour," *World Tennis*, vol. 35, no. 7, December 1987, p. 36.

3. Ross Wetzsteon, "I Was a Teenage U. S. Hope," *Sport*, vol. 80, no. 7, July 1989, p. 62.

4. Agassi, p. 36.

5. Sally Jenkins, "Love and Love," *Sports Illustrated*, vol. 82, no. 10, March 13, 1995, p. 57.

6. de Jonge, p. 77.

7. Ibid.

8. Jim Loehr, "Agassi's Mental Turnaround," *World Tennis*, vol. 36, no. 1 (June 1988), p. 40.

9. Gary Stern, *Andre Agassi: Tennis Prince* (Vero Beach, Fla.: Rourke Enterprises, Inc., 1993), p. 23.

10. Neil Amdur, "Stronger & Better," *World Tennis*, vol. 36, no. 1, June 1988, p. 38.

Chapter 5

1. Neil Amdur, "Stronger & Better," *World Tennis*, vol. 36, no. 1, June 1988, p. 36.

2. Curry Kirkpatrick, "Back From Exile," *Sports Illustrated*, vol. 69, no. 5, August 7, 1988, p. 41.

3. Ross Wetzsteon, "I Was a Teenage U.S. Hope," *Sport*, vol. 80, no. 7, July 1989, p. 64.

4. Amdur, p. 38.

5. Ross Wetzsteon, "The Age of Andre," *Sport*, vol. 80, no. 6, June 1989, p. 88.

6. Curry Kirkpatrick, "Special D from This Courier," *Sports Illustrated*, vol. 70, no. 25, June 12, 1989, p. 87.

7. Dave Scheiber, "Andre the Giant," *Sports Illustrated*, vol. 72, no. 14, April 2, 1990, p. 36.

8. Ibid, p. 37.

9. Wetzsteon, "Hope," p. 62.

10. Mark Bloom, "Running and Cycling and Weights, Oh My!," *World Tennis*, vol. 38, no. 1, June 1990, pp. 43–44.

11. Scheiber, p. 37.

Chapter 6

1. Bruce Newman, "Worth the Weight," *Sports Illustrated,* vol. 73, no. 22, November 26, 1990, p. 44.

2. Nora McCabe, "Burden of Proof," *World Tennis,* vol. 38, no. 9, February 1991, p. 71.

3. Ibid.

4. Ibid.

5. Curry Kirkpatrick, "Dustbusters," *Sports Illustrated,* vol. 73, no. 24, December 10, 1990, p. 45.

6. Curry Kirkpatrick, "It's Hammer Time," *Sports Illustrated,* vol. 74, no. 23, June 17, 1991, p. 35.

7. Sally Jenkins, "Love and Love," *Sports Illustrated,* vol. 82, no. 10, March 13, 1995, p. 57.

8. Newman, p. 44.

Chapter 7

1. Curry Kirkpatrick, "Agassi and Ecstasy," *Sports Illustrated,* vol. 77, no. 2, July 13, 1992, p. 19.

2. Sally Jenkins, "Image Is Not Everything," *Sports Illustrated,* vol. 76, no. 18, May 11, 1992, p. 37.

3. "Andre on the Rocks," *World Tennis,* vol. 38, no. 4, September 1990, p. 12.

4. Bruce Newman, "Worth the Weight," *Sports Illustrated,* vol. 73, no. 22, November 26, 1990, p. 44.

5. Jenkins, "Image," p. 37.

6. Sally Jenkins, "Comic Strip," *Sports Illustrated,* vol. 79, no. 1, July 5, 1993, p. 22.

7. Ibid.

8. *Sports Illustrated 1994 Sports Almanac* (Boston: Little, Brown and Company, 1994).

9. Sally Jenkins, "As Real As He Gets," *Sports Illustrated*, vol. 80, no. 12, March 28, 1994, p. 46.

10. Ibid, p. 51.

11. "Zen Master," *People*, vol. 41, no. 1, January 10, 1994, p. 35.

Chapter 8

1. "Agassi Comfortable With His New Lifestyle," *Los Angeles Times*, dispatch from Las Vegas, March 6, 1995.

2. Ibid.

3. Ibid.

4. Ibid.

5. S. L. Price, "Anarchy and Agassi," *Sports Illustrated*, vol. 81, no. 12, September 19, 1994, p. 39.

6. Sally Jenkins, "Love and Love," *Sports Illustrated*, vol. 82, no. 10, March 13, 1995, p. 59.

7. Ibid.

8. "She's Game, He's Set," *People*, vol. 42, no. 2, July 11, 1994, p. 98.

9. Jenkins, "Love," p. 58.

10. Robin Finn, "Agassi Plants Another Seed at the Open," *The New York Times*, September 8, 1994, p. B14.

11. Ibid.

12. Robin Finn, "Agassi the Upset King to Duel

With Stich," *The New York Times*, September 11, 1994, sec. 8, p. 1.

13. Ibid. sec. 8, p. 4.

14. Price, p. 34.

15. Robin Finn, "The New Agassi Style Now Has Substance," *The New York Times*, September 12, 1994, p. C1.

16. Harvey Araton, "A Grungy Showman: 'Uh, Wow!' and Cool," *The New York Times*, September 12, 1994, p. C3.

17. Price, p. 39.

18. "Andre Agassi," *People*, vol. 42, no. 26, December 26, 1994-January 2, 1995, p. 93.

Chapter 9

1. Sally Jenkins, "Love and Love," *Sports Illustrated*, vol. 82, no. 10, March 13, 1995, p. 54.

2. Emily Mitchell, "The Unkindest Cut of All," *Time*, January 30, 1995.

3. Sally Jenkins, "Beauty and Baldy," *Sports Illustrated*, vol. 82, no. 5, February 6, 1995, p. 46.

4. Ibid. p. 51.

5. Associated Press dispatch from Melbourne, Australia, January 29, 1995.

6. Associated Press dispatch from Pone Vedra Beach, April 11, 1995.

7. Ibid.

8. Ibid.

9. Associated Press dispatch from Tokyo, April 17, 1995.

10. Reuters dispatch from London, July 1995.

11. Associated Press dispatch from Montreal, July 31, 1995.

12. Ibid.

13. Associated Press dispatch from Mason, Ohio, August 14, 1995.

14. Doug Smith, "The Bandannas are Flying," *USA Today*, September 5, 1995, p. 8C.

15. Ibid.

16. Reuters dispatch from New York, August 21, 1995.

17. PR Newswire dispatch from New York, September 7, 1995.

18. Bob Cloud, "Agassi Serves up New Cafe," *Las Vegas Sun*, April 4, 1996, p. 1E.

19. Bill Berkrot, Reuters dispatch from Las Vegas, September 21, 1995.

20. Ibid.

21. Reuters dispatch from Key Biscayne, Florida, March 29, 1996.

22. Doug Smith, "Agassi Wins Lipton Title When Ivanisevic Defaults," *USA Today*, April 1, 1996, p. 12C.

23. Associated Press dispatch from Key Biscayne, Florida, March 31, 1996.

24. Reuters dispatch from London, April 4, 1996.

25. Doug Smith, "Bandannas," p. 8C.

Career Statistics

SINGLES

	Tournaments						Matches			
YEAR	TOT	W	F	S	Q	E	TOT	W	L	PCT.
1986	6	0	0	0	1	5	11	5	6	0.455
1987	18	1	1	2	2	12	43	26	17	0.605
1988	16	6	1	3	3	2	71	60	11	0.845
1989	16	1	1	5	2	6	54	37	17	0.685
1990	13	4	3	0	2	4	53	43	10	0.811
1991	18	2	1	2	4	9	53	36	17	0.679
1992	17	3	0	1	2	12	50	35	15	0.700
1993	13	2	0	2	4	5	43	32	11	0.744
1994	19	5	1	2	4	7	66	52	14	0.788
1995	16	7	4	2	2	1	80	71	9	0.888
1996	15	3	1	2	2	7	50	38	12	0.760
1997	12	0	0	1	1	10	22	10	12	0.455
1998	20	5	9	11	13	7	86	68	18	0.791
1999	18	5	8	12	14	4	77	63	14	0.818
2000	12	1	2	4	4	8	43	32	11	0.744
Total	229	45	32	49	60	99	802	608	194	0.758

Totals do not include Davis Cup competition.
Tot=Total, W=Win, F=Final, S=Semifinal, Q=Quarterfinal, E=Eliminated Earlier,L=Loss, Pct.=Percentage

Where to Write Andre Agassi

On the Internet at:

ATP Tour Homepage:
http://www.atptour.com/players/

ESPN's Agassi Profile:
http://espn.go.com/tennis/s/atp/profiles/agassi.htm

Index